# THREE GOOD REASONS FOR BUYING THIS BOOK:

"It is simply the most remarkable and entertaining collection of quotations ever compiled." — Edward McLachlan.

"The illustrations are hilarious and unique, the work of a genius at the height of his powers." — Roger Kilroy.

"In this life one should try everything once, except incest and folk-dancing." — Arnold Bax.

KISS ME, HARDY

Quotations ancient and modern.
Compiled and introduced by
ROGER KILROY

Illustrated by

McLACHLAN

KISS ME, HARDY

A CORGI BOOK 0 552 99006 X

First publication in Great Britain

PRINTING HISTORY
Corgi edition published 1982

Copyright © Roger Kilroy 1982
Illustrations © Ed McLachlan 1982

Corgi Books are published by
Transworld Publishers Ltd.,
Century House, 61-63 Uxbridge Road,
Ealing, London W5 5SA

Made and printed in Great Britain by the Guernsey Press Co. Ltd., Guernsey, Channel Islands.

# CONTENTS

# INTRODUCTION

I hate quotations. Tell me what you know.
— Ralph Waldo Emerson

What I know is that I love quotations and in the pages that follow I have collected — and the inimitable McLachlan has illustrated — all my favourites.

As you will see, they come in various shapes and sizes. There are long ones:

I always find that statistics are hard to swallow and impossible to digest. The only one I can ever remember is that if all the people who go to sleep in church were laid end to end they would be a lot more comfortable.
— Mrs. Robert A. Taft

And short ones:

Statistics are like a bikini. What they reveal is suggestive, but what they conceal is vital.
— Aaron Levenstein

Old ones:

Do not use a hatchet to remove a fly from your friend's forehead.
— Chinese Proverb

And new ones:

Airline travel is hours of boredom interrupted by moments of stark terror.
— Al Boliska

True ones:

If you don't learn to laugh at trouble, you won't have anything to laugh at when you grow old.
— Ed Howe

And terribly true ones:

> At no time is freedom of speech more precious than when a man
> hits his thumb with a hammer.
>
> — Marshall Lumsden

Familiar ones:

> There's a sucker born every minute.
>
> — P. T. Barnum

And less familiar ones:

> Testiculos habet et bene pendentes.
>
> — Pope Joan

(All translations, by the way, have been provided by experts. I'm no good
at Latin. For years I thought that **In loco Parentis** meant 'My dad's an
engine driver.')

Some of the quotations don't apply to McLachlan and me:

> There are books of which the backs and covers are by far the best
> parts.
>
> — Charles Dickens

> Posterity — what you write for after being turned down by
> publishers.
>
> — George Ade

But some do:

> I love criticism just so long as it's unqualified praise.
>
> — Noel Coward

You won't find 'Elementary, my dear Watson' here, both because
Sherlock Holmes **never** said it and because this isn't a dictionary of
quotations. It's an exploration of 'Life' in inverted commas. Indeed **Life**
is the title of one of the chapters because they all take their names from
magazines of one kind or another. Some — like **Life** and **Vogue** and
**Woman** — are well-known. Others are verging on the obscure. **Quest for
Success,** for example, is a monthly magazine for ambitious executives
published in Salt Lake City and **Use of English** is an educational journal
brought out three times a year in St. Albans. I thought I would be
stumped by X, Y and Z until I came across **XYZ**, 'the organ of the Mid-
Western Institute of Funeral Directors, Morticians and Embalmers'.
While there's death, there's hope.

The range of people quoted is very wide, from Woody Allen to Zsa Zsa Gabor, via Hitler, Snoopy and Oscar Wilde, who gets a whole chapter to himself: **Boy's Own.** (As his brother said: 'Oscar was not a man of bad character. You could trust him with a woman anywhere.') The first chapter **(Antiquity)** features the oldest quotes in the book. All the other chapters have a theme of their own. If you subscribe to **Golf World** then **Golf World's** a chapter you'll enjoy. If **Playboy** and **Men Only** are your staple fare, you should like the chapter called **Kinky.** If you're a devoted reader of the **Church Times,** you're probably in for a disappointment.

However, if you're a **Cosmopolitan** and like **Variety,** you should find plenty of **Punch** — and more than a little **Truth** — in the **Titbits** that follow.

**Readers, digest!**

ROGER KILROY.

# ANTIQUITY

WE ARE NOT AMUSED.
— Queen Victoria

There's time to win the game and thrash the Spaniards too.
— SIR FRANCIS DRAKE

# VENI, VIDI, VICI.
### —Julius Caesar

## To be or not to be, that is the question — HAMLET

# Workers of the world, unite!
### — KARL MARX

LET THEM EAT CAKE.
— Queen Marie Antoinette

cannot tell a lie. — GEORGE WASHINGTON

NOT TONIGHT, JOSEPHINE. — Napoleon

r. Livingstone, I presume.
— SIR HENRY STANLEY

FOOLS RUSH IN WHERE
ANGELS FEAR TO TREAD.
— Alexander Pope

# BOY'S OWN

TO LOVE ONESELF IS THE
BEGINNING OF A LIFELONG ROMANC
—Oscar Wilde

The only form of lying that is
absolutely beyond reproach
is lying for its own sake.
— OSCAR WILDE

There are people who say I have
never really done anything wrong
in my life; of course, they only say
it behind my back. —— OSCAR WILDE

YOUNG MEN WANT TO BE FAITHFUL AND AR
NOT; OLD MEN WANT TO BE FAITHLESS AND CANNO
— Oscar Wild

One must have a heart of stone to read the death of Little Nell without laughing. ———OSCAR WILDE

NIAGARA FALLS IS ONLY THE SECOND BIGGEST DISAPPOINTMENT OF THE STANDARD HONEYMOON. – Oscar Wilde

When I went to America I had two secretaries, one for autographs, the other for locks of hair. Within six months the one had died of writer's cramp, the other was completely bald.
— OSCAR WILDE

A cynic is a man who knows the price of everything and the value of nothing.

— OSCAR WILDE

PESSIMIST : ONE WHO, WHEN HE HAS THE CHOICE OF TWO EVILS, CHOOSES BOTH.

— OSCAR WILDE

If England treats her criminals the way she has treated me, she doesn't deserve to have any

— OSCAR WILDE

WHEN I WAS YOUNG I THOUGHT THAT MONEY WAS THE MOST IMPORTANT THING IN LIFE; NOW THAT I AM OLD I KNOW THAT IT IS! -

— OSCAR WILDE

# THE CONNOISSEUR

ABSTRACT ART: A product of the untalented, sold by the unprincipled to the utterly bewildered. —AL CAPP

Anyone who sees and paints a sky green and pastures blue ought to be sterilized! —ADOLF HITLER.

17

A PAINTER WHO HAS THE FEEL
OF BREASTS AND BUTTOCKS IS SAVED.
— Auguste Renoir

I DO NOT PAINT A PORTRAIT TO LOOK LIKE THE
SUBJECT, RATHER DOES THE PERSON GROW
TO LOOK LIKE HIS PORTRAIT — Salvador Dali

A painting in a museum hears more
ridiculous opinions than anything
else in the world.
— EDMOND DE GONCOURT

THE DERISIVE
CAVALIER

The English may not like music,
but they absolutely
love the sound it makes.
— SIR THOMAS BEECHAM

NO GOOD OPERA PLOT CAN BE
SENSIBLE, FOR PEOPLE DO NOT SING
WHEN THEY ARE FEELING SENSIBLE.
— W.H. Auden

Wagner's music
is better than
it sounds.
— MARK TWAIN

A POET IN HISTORY IS DIVINE,
BUT A POET IN THE NEXT ROOM
IS A JOKE – Max Eastman

Music and women
I cannot but give way to,
whatever my business is.
— SAMUEL PEPYS

# DECANTER

A WOMAN DROVE ME TO DRINK AND I NEVER EVEN HAD THE COURTESY TO THANK HER. —— W.C. Fields

What contemptible scoundrel stole the cork from my lunch? — W.C. FIELDS

I ALWAYS KEEP A SUPPLY OF STIMULANT HANDY IN CASE I SEE A SNAKE — WHICH I ALSO KEEP HANDY. — W.C. Fields

Anyone who hates dogs and loves whisky can't be all bad. — W.C. FIELDS

HE TALKED
WITH MORE
CLARET THAN
CLARITY.
—Susan Ertz

I DRINK TO
MAKE OTHER
PEOPLE
INTERESTING.
—George Jean Nathan

When I sell liquor,
it's called bootlegging;
when my patrons serve
it on silver trays
on Lake Shore Drive,
it's called hospitality.
— AL CAPONE

# THE ECONOMIST

It doesn't matter if you're rich
or poor, as long as you've got money.
— JOE E. LEWIS

IF ONLY GOD WOULD GIVE ME SOME
CLEAR SIGN! LIKE MAKING A LARGE
DEPOSIT IN MY NAME AT A SWISS BANK.
— Woody Allen

The rich man and his daughter
are soon parted.
— FRANK McKINNEY

I'D LIKE TO LIVE LIKE A POOR MAN WITH
WITH LOTS OF MONEY. — Pablo Picasso

Pigasso

NOTHING IS MORE ADMIRABLE
THAN THE FORTITUDE WITH WHICH
MILLIONAIRES TOLERATE THE
DISADVANTAGES OF THEIR WEALTH
—— Rex Stout

To be clever enough to get a great
deal of money, one must be stupid
enough to want it. —— G.K.CHESTERTON

**He had so much money
that he could afford
to look poor.** —— EDGAR WALLACE

A banker is a person who is willing to make a loan if you present sufficient evidence to show you don't need it.
— HERBERT V. PROCHNOW

I'VE BEEN RICH AND I'VE BEEN POOR — RICH IS BETTER.
— Sophie Tucker

If you don't want to work you have to earn enough money so that you won't have to work. — OGDEN NASH

FIRST SECURE AN INDEPENDENT INCOME, THEN PRACTICE VIRTUE — Greek Proverb

Nowadays, two can live as cheaply as one large family used to!
— JOEY ADAMS

NEVER INVEST YOUR MONEY IN ANYTHING THAT EATS OR NEEDS REPAIRING — Billy Rose

The safest way to double your money is to fold it over once and put it back in your pocket. — FRANK McKINNEY HUBBARD

WEALTH — ANY INCOME THAT IS AT LEAST ONE HUNDRED DOLLARS MORE A YEAR THAN THE INCOME OF ONE'S WIFE'S SISTER'S HUSBAND.
— H.L.Mencken

# FAMILY CIRCLE

Marriage is a great institution,
but I'm not ready for an institution yet.
— MAE WEST

When singleness is bliss,
it's folly to be wives.
— BILL COUNSELMAN

A MAN IN LOVE IS INCOMPLETE UNTIL
HE HAS MARRIED. THEN HE'S FINISHED.
— Zsa Zsa Gabor

MARRIAGE: A COMMUNITY CONSISTING OF
A MASTER, A MISTRESS, AND TWO SLAVES—
— MAKING TWO IN ALL. —— Ambrose Bierce

ALL MARRIAGES ARE HAPPY. IT'S THE LIVING TOGETHER AFTERWARD THAT CAUSES ALL THE TROUBLE –Raymond Hul

**Matrimony is a process by which a grocer acquired an account the florist had.**
—FRANCIS RODMAN

The most popular labour-saving
device today is still a husband with money.
— JOEY ADAMS

SHE SAID HE PROPOSED SOMETHING ON
THEIR WEDDING NIGHT HER OWN BROTHER
WOULDN'T HAVE SUGGESTED.
— James Thurber

Marriage is the deep, deep peace
of the double bed after the hurly-burly
of the chaise longue — MRS. PATRICK CAMPBELL

Memory is what tells a man
that his wife's birthday
was yesterday. — MARIO ROCCO

I AM A MARVELLOUS HOUSEKEEPER.
EVERY TIME I LEAVE A MAN,
I KEEP HIS HOUSE. — Zsa Zsa Gabor

There is one thing more exasperating
than a wife who can cook and won't,
and that's the wife who can't cook and will!
— ROBERT FROST.

29

I HAVEN'T KNOWN ANY OPEN MARRIAGES THOUGH QUITE A FEW HAVE BEEN AJAR.
———— Bob Hope

Did you hear about the fellow who blamed arithmetic for his divorce? His wife put two and two together. ———— EARL WILSON

WIFE BEATING MAY BE SOCIALLY ACCEPTABLE IN SHEFFIELD, BUT IT IS A DIFFERENT MATTER IN CHELTENHAM ———— Lord Justice Lawton

# GOLF WORLD

IF YOU WATCH A GAME, IT'S FUN.
IF YOU PLAY IT, IT'S RECREATION.
IF YOU WORK AT IT, IT'S GOLF.
——Bob Hope

Have you ever noticed
what golf spells backwards?
——AL BOLISKA

GOLF IS LIKE A LOVE AFFAIR: IF YOU
DON'T TAKE IT SERIOUSLY, IT'S NO FUN;
IF YOU DO TAKE IT SERIOUSLY, IT BREAKS
YOUR HEART. ——Arnold Daly

Golf is a good walk spoiled —MARK TWAIN

JOGGING IS VERY BENEFICIAL.
IT'S GOOD FOR YOUR LEGS AND
YOUR FEET. IT'S ALSO VERY GOOD
FOR THE GROUND. IT MAKES
IT FEEL NEEDED. —— Snoopy

A woman who has never seen her
husband fishing doesn't know what
a patient man she has married.
—— ED HOWE

If you
drink,
don't drive
Don't even
putt!
—— DEAN MARTIN

# HERE'S HEALTH

All the things I really like to do are either immoral, illegal or fattening. — ALEXANDER WOOLLCOTT

DIETS ARE FOR THOSE WHO ARE THICK AND TIRED OF IT.
— Mary Tyler Moore

The other day I got on a weighing machine that stamps your weight on a card. When the card came out, it said, 'Come back in ten minutes — alone.'
— JACKIE GLEASON

DIET — A SYSTEM OF STARVING YOURSELF TO DEATH SO YOU CAN LIVE A LITTLE LONGER
— Totie Fields

MOST OF THE TIME I DON'T
HAVE MUCH FUN. THE REST OF
THE TIME I DON'T HAVE ANY
FUN AT ALL. —— Woody Allen

The unfortunate thing about
this world is that good habits
are so much easier to give up
than bad ones. —— SOMERSET MAUGHAM

I GOT THE BILL FOR MY SURGERY.
NOW I KNOW WHAT THOSE DOCTORS WERE
WEARING MASKS FOR.
—James Boren

If God meant us to eat sugar
he wouldn't have invented dentists.
— RALPH NADER

To the person with a
toothache, even if the
world is tottering, there
is nothing more important
than a visit to a dentist.
— GEORGE BERNARD SHAW

WHEN CHOOSING BETWEEN TWO EVILS,
I ALWAYS LIKE TO TRY THE ONE I'VE
NEVER TRIED BEFORE — Mae West

To cease smoking is the easiest thing
I ever did. I ought to know
because I've done it
a thousand times.
— MARK TWAIN

HE FINALLY
GAVE UP
SMOKING

# Iɴᴛᴇʀɴᴀᴛɪᴏɴᴀʟ ᴀꜰꜰᴀɪʀꜱ

A diplomat is a person who can tell you to go to hell in such a way that you actually look forward to the trip. —CASKIE STINNETT

DIPLOMACY IS THE ART OF SAYING 'NICE DOGGIE!' TILL YOU CAN FIND A ROCK. —Wynn Catlin

Diplomacy—the patriotic art of lying for one's country
—AMBROSE BIERCE

THERE ARE A TERRIBLE LOT OF LIES GOING ROUND THE WORLD, AND THE WORST OF IT IS THAT HALF OF THEM ARE TRUE. — Winston Churchill

**You cannot shake hands with a clenched fist.**
—— INDIRA GANDHI

You can get much farther with a kind word and a gun than you can with a kind word alone. —————— AL CAPONE

A POLITICAL WAR IS ONE IN WHICH EVERYONE SHOOTS FROM THE LIP.
—— Raymond Moley

YOU CAN'T SAY THAT CIVILIZATION DOESN'T ADVANCE, FOR IN EVERY WAR THEY KILL YOU A NEW WAY.
— Will Rogers

COWARD: A man in whom the instinct of self-preservation acts normally — SULTANA ZORAYA

# JUSTICE

THE LAW, IN ITS MAJESTIC EQUALITY,
FORBIDS THE RICH AS WELL AS THE POOR
TO SLEEP UNDER BRIDGES, TO BEG IN THE
STREETS AND TO STEAL BREAD.
                    — Anatole France

If some people got their rights
they would complain of being
deprived of their wrongs.
                    — OLIVER HERTFORD

LAWS ARE SPIDER WEBS
THROUGH WHICH THE BIG
FLIES PASS AND THE LITTLE
ONES GET CAUGHT.
    — Honoré de Balzac

HONESTY : THE MOST IMPORTANT THING IN LIFE. UNLESS YOU REALLY KNOW HOW TO FAKE IT, YOU'LL NEVER MAKE IT. —Bernard Rosenberg

There's one way to find if a man is honest — ask him.
If he says, 'Yes,' you know he's a crook. —— GROUCHO MARX

No doubt Jack the Ripper excused himself on the grounds that it was human nature. —A.A. MILNE

But nobody knows (tiddely pom)

# KINKY

One must not lose one's desires. They are mighty stimulants to creativeness, to love, and to long life.
— ALEXANDER A. BOGOMOLETZ

In sexual intercourse it's quality not quantity that counts — DR. DAVID REUBEN

MAKE LOVE TO EVERY WOMAN YOU MEET; IF YOU GET FIVE PERCENT ON YOUR OUTLAYS IT'S A GOOD INVESTMENT
— ARNOLD BENNETT

HE WAS ONE OF THOSE MEN WHO
COME IN A DOOR AND MAKE ANY
WOMAN WITH THEM LOOK GUILTY.
——F. SCOTT FITZGERALD

If I told you you have a beautiful
body, you wouldn't hold it against
me would you? —— DAVID FISHER

SHE WAS THE ORIGINAL
GOOD TIME THAT WAS
HAD BY ALL —Bette Davis

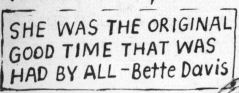

Give a
man a
free hand
and he'll
run it all
over you.
—— MAE WEST

Whoever named it necking
was a poor judge of anatomy.
— GROUCHO MARX

IT DOESN'T MATTER WHAT YOU DO
IN THE BEDROOM AS LONG AS YOU DON'T
DO IT IN THE STREET & FRIGHTEN THE HORSES.
— Mrs. Patrick Campbell

Variety is the spice of sex.
— MARABEL MORGAN

AMONG THE PORCUPINES, RAPE IS UNKNOWN
— Gregory Clark

Continental people have sex lives;
the English have hot water bottles.
— GEORGE MIKES

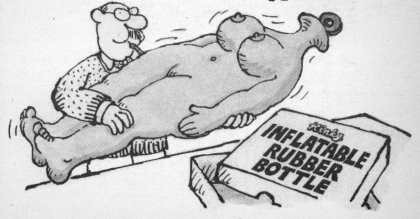

INFLATABLE
RUBBER
BOTTLE

I WASN'T REALLY NAKED.
I SIMPLY DIDN'T HAVE ANY CLOTHES ON.
— Josephine Baker

Men aren't attracted to me by
my mind. They're attracted
by what I don't mind.
— Gypsy Rose Lee

If I hadn't had them,
I would have had some made
— DOLLY PARTON

# LIFE

LIFE IS LIKE PLAYING A VIOLIN IN PUBLIC AND LEARNING THE INSTRUMENT AS ONE GOES ON —Samuel Butler

Life is what happens to us while we are making other plans. —THOMAS LA MANCE

MY GRANDFATHER ALWAYS SAID THAT LIVING IS LIKE LICKING HONEY OFF A THORN.
—Louis Adamic

SHAKE AND SHAKE
THE KETCHUP BOTTLE,
NONE WILL COME,
AND THEN A LOT'LL
—Richard Armour

My life has no purpose,
no direction, no aim, no meaning,
and yet I'm happy. I can't figure
it out. What am I doing right?
— CHARLES M. SCHULZ

EXPERIENCE : A comb life gives you
after you lose your hair.
— JUDITH STERN

NOT A SHRED OF EVIDENCE
EXISTS IN FAVOUR OF THE
IDEA THAT LIFE IS SERIOUS.
— Brendan Gill

The optimist proclaims that we live in the best of all possible worlds, and the pessimist fears this is true
—JAMES BRANCH CABELL

MULTI-STOREY CAR PARK

A PESSIMIST IS A MAN WHO LOOKS BOTH WAYS BEFORE CROSSING A ONE-WAY STREET.
—Laurence J. Peter

NOTHING MAKES YOU MORE
TOLERANT OF A NEIGHBOUR'S NOISY
PARTY THAN BEING THERE.
——Franklin P. Jones

Love thy neighbour
as thyself — but choose
your neighbourhood.
—LOUISE BEA

A tourist is a fellow who drives thousands of miles so he can be photographed standing in front of his car.———— EMILE GANEST

MILLIONS LONG FOR IMMORTALITY WHO DO NOT KNOW WHAT TO DO WITH THEMSELVES ON A RAINY SUNDAY AFTERNOON.
———— Susan Ertz

The trouble with being punctual is that nobody's there to appreciate it. — FRANKLIN P. JONES

NEVER LEARN TO DO ANYTHING: IF YOU DON'T LEARN, YOU'LL ALWAYS FIND SOMEONE ELSE TO DO IT FOR YOU.
———— Mark Twain

A perpetual holiday is a good working definition of hell.
— GEORGE BERNARD SHAW

THE TROUBLE WITH THE RAT RACE IS THAT EVEN IF YOU WIN, YOU'RE STILL A RAT! — Lily Tomlin

Retirement at sixty-five is ridiculous. When I was sixty-five I still had pimples. — GEORGE BURNS

The reason why worry kills more people than work is that more people worry than work.
— ROBERT FROST

WHEN A MAN RETIRES AND TIME IS NO LONGER A MATTER OF URGENT IMPORTANCE, HIS COLLEAGUES GENERALLY PRESENT HIM WITH A WATCH.
— R. C. Sherriff

A lot of fellows nowadays have a B.A., an M.D. or a Ph.D.. Unfortunately they don't have a J.O.B. —— FATS DOMINO

THE CLOSEST TO PERFECTION A PERSON EVER COMES, IS WHEN HE FILLS OUT A JOB APPLICATION FORM.
Stanley J. Randall

MAN — A creature made at thet end of the week's work when God was tired. — MARK TWAIN

MOST OF THE EVILS OF LIFE ARISE FROM MAN'S INABILITY TO SIT STILL IN A ROOM — Blaise Pascal

The more I see of man, the more I like dogs.
— MME DE STAËL

# MANAGEMENT TODAY

COMMITTEE — A GROUP OF MEN WHO
INDIVIDUALLY CAN DO NOTHING BUT
AS A GROUP DECIDE THAT NOTHING
CAN BE DONE. —— Fred Allen

Committee — a group of men who
keep minutes and waste hours.
                    — MILTON BERLE

You'll find in no park or city
A monument to a committee.
            — VICTORIA PASTERNAK

# NURSERY WORLD

IF YOUR PARENTS DIDN'T HAVE ANY CHILDREN, THERE'S A GOOD CHANCE THAT YOU WON'T HAVE ANY EITHER
— Clarence Day

The first half of our life is ruined by our parents and the second half by our children.
— CLARENCE DARROW

You can learn many things from children.— How much patience you have, for instance.

— FRANKLIN P. JONES

WE ALL WORRY ABOUT THE POPULATION EXPLOSION — BUT WE DON'T ALL WORRY ABOUT IT AT THE RIGHT TIME – Arthur Hoppe

My mother loved children —she would have given anything if I had been one.

— GROUCHO MARX

MUMBLE GRUNT SLOBBER

Whenever I hear people discussing birth control, I always remember that I was the fifth.

— CLARENCE DARROW

THERE ARE TWO CLASSES OF TRAVEL
— FIRST CLASS AND WITH CHILDREN.
— Robert Benchley

**PRODIGY: A child who plays the piano when he ought to be asleep in bed.**
—J. B. MORTON

The modern child will answer you back before you've said anything.
— LAURENCE J. PETER

THE THING THAT IMPRESSES ME MOST ABOUT AMERICA IS THE WAY PARENTS OBEY THEIR CHILDREN.
—The Duke of Windsor

Insanity is hereditary; ou can get from your children.
—SAM LEVENSON

he best way to keep children ome is to make the home atmos- here happy— and let the air out f the tyres.—— DOROTHY PARKER

CHILDREN ARE A GREAT COMFORT J YOUR OLD AGE — AND THEY HELP OU REACH IT FASTER, TOO.
——Lionel Kauffman

MOST PARENTS DON'T WORRY
ABOUT A DAUGHTER UNTIL SHE FAILS
TO SHOW UP FOR BREAKFAST.......
— THEN IT IS TOO LATE.
                    Frank McKinney Hubbard

**YOUTHQUAKE: An eruption
followed by a twitch, a tic,
and a much sullen or
ashen silence.**
—BERNARD ROSENBERG

...and then
permanent
silence

# OVER 21

You grow up the day you have the first real laugh—at yourself.
— ETHEL BARRYMORE

A man is only as old as the woman he feels. — GROUCHO MARX

A MAN BEGINS CUTTING HIS WISDOM TEETH THE FIRST TIME HE BITES OFF MORE THAN HE CAN CHEW. —————— Herb Caen

YOU'VE HEARD OF THE THREE AGES OF MAN: YOUTH, MIDDLE AGE, AND 'YOU'RE LOOKING WONDERFUL'.
— Cardinal Spellman

Growing old isn't so bad when you consider the alternative.
— MAURICE CHEVALIER

**I am in the prime of senility.** JOEL CHANDLER HARR

YOU KNOW YOU'RE GETTING OLD WHEN THE CANDLES COST MORE THAN THE CAKE ——— Bob Hope

I'm sixty-five and I guess that put me in with the geriatrics, but if there were fifteen months in every year, I'd only be forty-eight — JAMES THURBER

OF LATE I APPEAR
TO HAVE REACHED THAT STAGE,
WHEN PEOPLE LOOK OLD
WHO ARE ONLY MY AGE. —Richard Armour

MIDDLE AGE IS WHEN YOUR OLD CLASSMATES ARE SO GREY, WRINKLED AND BALD THEY DON'T RECOGNISE YOU.
— Bennet Cerf

Middle Age is when your age starts to show around your middle. — BOB HOPE

MIDDLE AGE IS WHEN YOU'RE SITTING AT HOME ON SATURDAY NIGHT AND THE TELEPHONE RINGS AND YOU ANXIOUSLY HOPE IT ISN'T FOR YOU! — Ogden Nash

Middle Age — When a man is warned to slow down by a doctor instead of a policeman — SIDNEY BRODY

LIFE WOULD BE INFINITELY HAPPIER
IF WE COULD ONLY BE BORN AT THE
AGE OF EIGHTY AND THEN TO
GRADUALLY APPROACH EIGHTEEN.
—Mark Twain

There's no fool like an old fool.
you can't beat experience.
—JACOB M. BRAUDE

Grandchildren don't make a man
feel old; it's the knowledge that
he's married to
a grandmother.
—G. NORMAN COLLIE

Old people love to give good advice;
it compensates them for their
inability to set a bad example.
—Duc de la Rochefocauld

FIRST YOU FORGET NAMES, THEN YOU
FORGET FACES, THEN YOU FORGET TO
PULL YOUR ZIP UP, THEN YOU FORGET
TO PULL YOUR ZIP DOWN.
— Leo Rosenberg

An archeologist is the best husband
any woman can have;
the older she gets,
the more interested
he is in her.
—AGATHA CHRISTIE.

# PSYCHIATRY TODAY

A PSYCHIATRIST IS A FELLOW WHO ASKS YOU A LOT OF EXPENSIVE QUESTIONS YOUR WIFE ASKS FOR NOTHING.
——Joey Adams

Anyone who goes to a psychiatrist ought to have his head examined.
—— Samuel Goldwyn

A NEUROTIC IS A MAN WHO BUILDS A CASTLE IN THE AIR. A PSYCHOTIC IS THE MAN WHO LIVE IN IT. A PSYCHIATRIST IS THE MAN WHO COLLECTS THE RENT.—Jerome Lawrence

A psychiatrist is a man who goes to the Folies-Bergère and looks at the audience.—— MERVYN STOCKWOOD

TELL US YOUR PHOBIAS AND WE
WILL TELL YOU WHAT YOU ARE AFRAID OF.
— Robert Benchley

# I am free of all prejudices.
# I hate every one equally.
— W.C. FIELDS

Jack Sprat could eat no fat,
His wife could eat no lean.
A real sweet pair of neurotics.
——JACK SHARKEY

THE **S**UPEREGO IS THAT PART OF THE
PERSONALITY WHICH IS SOLUBLE IN ALCOHOL.
——Professor Harold Lasswell

A little madness in the Spring
Is wholesome, even for the King.
— EMILY DICKINSON

## We are all born mad. Some remain so.
— SAMUEL BECKETT

ONE OUT OF FOUR PEOPLE IN THIS
COUNTRY IS MENTALLY IMBALANCED.
THINK OF YOUR THREE CLOSEST
FRIENDS — AND IF THEY SEEM OKAY
THEN YOU'RE THE ONE! — Ann Landers

# QUEST FOR SUCCESS

THE TWO LEADING RECIPES FOR
SUCCESS ARE BUILDING A BETTER
MOUSETRAP AND FINDING A BIGGER LOOPHOLE.
— Edgar A. Shoaff

I cannot give you the formula
for success but I can give you the
formula for failure — which is:
Try to please everybody!
— Herbert Bayard Swope

To escape criticism —
  do nothing, say nothing,
    be nothing.
— ELBERT HUBBARD

IF AT FIRST YOU DON'T SUCCEED,
TRY, TRY AGAIN. THEN QUIT. THERE'S
NO USE BEING A DAMN FOOL ABOUT IT.
— W. C. Fields

WHEN A MAN BLAMES OTHERS FOR HIS FAILURES, IT'S A GOOD IDEA TO CREDIT OTHERS WITH HIS SUCCESSES.
— Howard W. Newton

A doctor can bury his mistakes but an architect can only advise his client to plant vines.
— Frank Lloyd Wright

I HAVE GREAT FAITH IN FOOLS; SELF-CONFIDENCE MY FRIENDS CALL IT — Edgar Allan Poe

Crank — A man with a new idea.... until it succeeds — MARK TWAIN

The fellow who never makes
a mistake takes his orders from
one who does. ——Herbert V. Prochnow

ONLY A MEDIOCRE PERSON IS
ALWAYS AT HIS BEST. —Laurence Peter

The middle of the road is where
the line is — and that's the worst
place to drive — ROBERT FROST

YOU WON'T SKID
IF YOU STAY IN A RUT.
—Frank McKinney Hubbard

LET US BE THANKFUL FOR THE
FOOLS. BUT FOR THEM THE REST
OF US COULD NOT SUCCEED.
— Mark Twain

Experience enables you to
recognise a mistake when you
make it again.—FRANKLIN P. JONES

**Success is simply
a matter of luck—
Ask any failure.**
—EARL WILSON

BE AWFUL NICE TO 'EM GOING UP,
BECAUSE YOU'RE GOING TO MEET
'EM ALL COMING DOWN!
—— Jimmy Durante

# ROMANCE

Love doesn't make the world go round. Love is what makes the ride worthwhile.— FRANKLIN P. JONES

IF TWO PEOPLE LOVE EACH OTHER THERE CAN BE NO HAPPY END TO IT.
— Ernest Hemingway

It was not the apple on the tree, but the pair on the ground, I believe, that caused the trouble in the garden.
— M. D. O'CONNOR

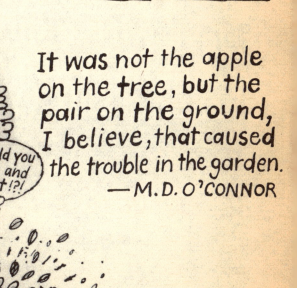

PLATONIC FRIENDSHIP:
THE INTERVAL BETWEEN THE
INTRODUCTION AND THE FIRST KISS.
      —Sophie Irene Loeb

Many a man has fallen
in love with a girl in a light
so dim he would not have
chosen a suit by it.
                —MAURICE CHEVALIER

Women are a problem, but if you haven't already guessed, they're the kind of problem I enjoy wrestling with.
——WARREN BEATTY

ONCE THEY CALL YOU A LATIN LOVER YOU'RE IN REAL TROUBLE. WOMEN EXPECT AN OSCAR PERFORMANCE IN BED.
— Marcello Mastroianni

I'm a practicing heterosexual.....
but bisexuality immediately doubles your chances for a date on Saturday night — WOODY ALLEN

A MAN WHO WON'T LIE TO A WOMAN HAS VERY LITTLE CONSIDERATION FOR HER FEELINGS —— Olin Miller

It's not the men in my life that counts — It's the life in my men.
——MAE WEST

KISSING YOUR HAND MAY
MAKE YOU FEEL GOOD, BUT A
DIAMOND AND SAPPHIRE BRACELET
LASTS FOR EVER. — Anita Loos

I never hated a man enough to
give him his diamonds back.
— Zsa Zsa Gabor

I DON'T LIKE HER. BUT DON'T
MISUNDERSTAND ME: MY DISLIKE
IS PURELY PLATONIC.-
— Sir Herbert Beerbohm Tre

Never let a fool kiss you or
a kiss fool you. —JOEY ADAMS

I HAVE ALWAYS THOUGHT OF A
DOG LOVER AS A DOG THAT WAS IN
LOVE WITH ANOTHER DOG.
— James Thurber

# Screen International

Hollywood is a place where the inmates are in charge of the asylum.
— LAURENCE STALLINGS

A CELEBRITY IS A PERSON WHO WORKS HARD ALL HIS LIFE TO BECOME WELL KNOWN, AND WEARS DARK GLASSES TO AVOID BEING RECOGNISED. — Fred Allen

A fan club is a group of people who tell an actor he's not alone in the way he feels about himself. — JACK CARSON

TV – chewing gum for the eyes.
— FRANK LLOYD WRIGHT

DO YOU REALISE IF IT WEREN'T FOR EDISON WE'D BE WATCHING TV BY CANDLELIGHT? — Al Boliska

Poor reception is about the only way you can improve some television programmes.
— Franklin P. Jones

HERE IS A VERY SERIOUS ANNOUNCEMENT......

TELEVISION HAS CHANGED THE MODERN CHILD FROM AN IRRESISTIBLE FORCE INTO A IMMOVABLE OBJECT. — Lawrence Peter

Television has proved that people will look at anything rather than each other. — ANN LANDERS

TELEVISION IS FOR APPEARING ON, NOT LOOKING AT. — Noël Coward

♪ A globe with a view and yo-ou... ♪♪♫

# **T**RIBUNE

POLITICS IS PERHAPS THE ONLY
PROFESSION FOR WHICH NO PREPARATIO
IS THOUGHT NECESSARY.
—Robert Louis Stevenso

> He knows nothing; he thinks he
> knows everything — that clearly
> points to a political career.
> — GEORGE BERNARD SHA

Since a politician never believes what he says, he is always astonished when others do. —CHARLES DE GAULLE

WHEN I WAS A BOY I WAS TOLD THAT ANYBODY COULD BECOME PRESIDENT OF THE UNITED STATES; I'M BEGINNING TO BELIEVE IT. —— Clarence Darrow

Politicians are the same all over. They promise to build a bridge even where there is no river.
—— NIKITA KHRUSCHEV

# USE OF ENGLISH

Adam was the only man who, when he said a good thing, knew that nobody had said it before him

— MARK TWAIN

NO MAN WOULD LISTEN TO YOU TALK IF HE DIDN'T KNOW IT WAS HIS TURN NEX

— Ed Howe

The trouble with her is that she lacks the power of conversation but not the power of speech.

— George Bernard Sha

DON'T TALK ABOUT YOURSELF;
IT WILL BE DONE WHEN YOU LEAVE.
—Wilson Mizner

Repartee: what a person thinks of
after he becomes a departee.
—DAN BENNETT

IF YOU THINK BEFORE YOU SPEAK, THE
OTHER FELLOW GETS IN HIS JOKE FIRST.
— Ed Howe

TACT: Ability to tell a man
he's open-minded when he has
a hole in his head — F. G. KERNAN

A bore is a man who, when you ask him how he is, tells you.
— BERT LESTON TAYLOR

HE IS AN OLD BORE; EVEN THE GRAVE YAWNS FOR HIM!
— Sir Herbert Beerbohm Tree

Every improvement in communication makes the bore more terrible.
— FRANK MOORE COLBY

A BORE IS A PERSON WHO TALKS WHEN YOU WANT HIM TO LISTEN.
— Ambrose Bierce

DRONE

HE IS A FINE FRIEND. HE STABS YOU IN THE FRONT. — Leonard Louis Levinson

**No call alligator big mouth till you pass him.** — JAMAICAN PROVERB

No one can have a higher opinion of him than I have — and I think he is a dirty little beast!
— W.S. GILBERT

JOURNALISM IS THE ABILITY
TO MEET THE CHALLENGE
OF FILLING SPACE.
— Rebecca West

The word 'good' has many
meanings. For example, if a man
were to shoot his grandmother
at a range of five hundred yards,
I should call him a good shot, but
not necessarily a good man.
— G.K. CHESTERTON

GOOD MAN!

# VOGUE

It's a good thing that beauty is only skin deep, or I'd be rotten to the core. —PHYLLIS DILLER

## When the candles are out, all women are fair
— PLUTARCH

SHE GOT HER GOOD LOOKS FROM HER FATHER.
— HE'S A PLASTIC SURGEON.
—Groucho Marx

And this is Jane 12 months ago

It's an ill wind that blows when you leave the hairdresser.
— PHYLLIS DILLER

If truth is beauty, how come no one has their hair done in the library? — LILY TOMLIN

REMEMBER ALWAYS THAT THE LEAST PLAIN SISTER IS THE FAMILY BEAUTY.
— GEORGE BERNARD SHAW

# WOMAN

THERE ARE ONLY TWO KINDS OF
WOMEN — GODDESSES AND DOORMATS.
— Pablo Picasso

I like men to behave like men
....strong and childish!
— FRANÇOISE SAGAN

A WOMAN HAS TO BE TWICE AS GOOD
AS A MAN TO GO HALF AS FAR.
— Fannie Hurst

When men reach their sixties and
retire, they go to pieces.
Women just go right on cooking.
— GAIL SHEEHY

BEHIND EVERY GREAT MAN IS A
WOMAN. AND BEHIND HER
IS HIS WIFE. — Groucho Marx

The only time a woman wishes she
were a year older is when she is
expecting a baby. — MARY MARSH

To my embarrassment I was born in bed with a lady.
— WILSON MIZNER

WOMEN WOULD BE THE MOST ENCHANTING CREATURES ON EARTH IF, IN FALLING INTO THEIR ARMS ONE DIDN'T FALL INTO THEIR HANDS!
— Eddie Fisher

CONTRARY TO POPULAR BELIEF, ENGLISH WOMEN DO NOT WEAR TWEED NIGHTGOWNS. — Hermione Gingold

DESPITE MY THIRTY YEARS OF
RESEARCH INTO THE FEMININE SOUL,
I HAVE NOT BET BEEN ABLE TO
ANSWER...THE GREAT QUESTION THAT
HAS NEVER BEEN ANSWERED:
WHAT DOES A WOMAN WANT?
— Sigmund Freud

A gentlemen is any man who
wouldn't hit a woman with his hat on.
— FRED ALLEN

I don't mind living in a man's world as long as I can be a woman in it.
— MARILYN MONROE

# A woman's place is in the wrong.

—JAMES THURBE

I asked a Burmese why women, after centuries of following their men now walk in front. He said there were many unexploded land mines since the war.
——ROBERT MUELLER

# XYZ

EVERY MAN OF GENIUS IS
CONSIDERABLY HELPED BY BEING DEAD.
— Robert S. Lynd

Every society honours
its live conformists and
its dead troublemakers.
— MIGMON McLAUGHLIN

IMMORTALITY
— A FATE WORSE THAN DEATH.
- Edgar A. Shoaff

I don't want to achieve immortality
through my work, I want to achieve
it through not dying!
— WOODY ALLEN

I'm not afraid to die. I just don't want to be there when it happens. —— WOODY ALLEN

A CYNIC IS A MAN WHO, WHEN HE SMELLS FLOWERS, LOOKS AROUND FOR A COFFIN. —— H. L. MENCKEN

A single death is a tragedy, a million deaths is a statistic.
—JOSEPH STALIN

Statistics, Shmatistics.

F I COULD DROP DEAD RIGHT NOW,
'D BE THE HAPPIEST MAN ALIVE!
                    — Samuel Goldwyn

# Only the young die good.
                    —OLIVER HERFORD

I have never wanted to see
nybody die, but there are a few
bituary notices I have read
vith pleasure. — CLARENCE DARROW

THE GOOD DIE YOUNG—BECAUSE
HEY SEE IT'S NO USE LIVING IF
OU'VE GOT TO BE GOOD.
                    —— John Barrymore

What a pity that the only
way to heaven is in a hearse!
— STANISLAW J. LEC

Nobody ever died of laughter.
— MAX BEERBOHM

The only completely consistent
people are the dead.
—ALDOUS HUXLEY

NO JOKING

If you're not allowed to
laugh in heaven, I don't want
to go there —MARTIN LUTHER

WHEN I LOOK BACK ON ALL THESE WORRIES I REMEMBER THE STORY OF THE OLD MAN WHO SAID ON HIS DEATHBED THAT HE HAD HAD A LOT OF TROUBLE IN HIS LIFE, MOST OF WHICH NEVER HAPPENED.
— Winston Churchill

---

If after I depart this vale, you ever remember me and have thought to please my ghost, forgive some sinner and wink your eye at some homely girl.
—H. L. MENCKEN

Since we have to speak well of the dead, let's knock them while they're alive —JOHN SLOAN

Wham! Wham! Wham!
Wham! Wham! Wham!
Wham! Wham! Wham!
Pop! Pop!

—MUHAMMED ALI

Ow! Ow! Ow!
Ow! Ow! Ow!
Ow! Ow! Ow!
Tweet! Tweet!